Contents

QUILTS

# Introduction

We love designing quilt patterns and being able to share our patterns with other quilters is a real joy. For us, quilts that are quick to make is key. This maybe stems from having to make numerous samples for our quilt shop! We have written and designed many jelly roll quilt patterns and our books have sold over 350,000 copies worldwide so don't think for a moment we have fallen out of love with jelly rolls. You will see that a number of jelly roll quilts have popped into this book as well - how did that happen! All the quilts in this book start with strips - although strips of many different widths.

Designing quilts that are quick to make sounds easy doesn't it? In truth, it can actually be very challenging. You want a quilt that doesn't take too long to make but one that looks fabulous and creative. You need it to look far more complicated than it really is and this is where clever techniques and the use of clever quilting rulers come into play.

We are always open minded and relish innovative quilting ideas and techniques. Quilting always remains a learning experience and we are still learning. This is great as it keeps everything new and fresh.

One of the units that has been popular for a long time and continues to be well loved and cherished is the flying geese unit. This unit features in many blocks to create exciting quilts and this is what our pattern book is all about. To create this unit we use the Creative Grids Multi-Size Flying Geese & 45°/90° Triangle (Creative Grids code CGRMSFG4590).

When we design quilt patterns we choose the rulers we use very carefully. We want rulers that are able to achieve numerous design possibilities and rulers that are going to stand the test of time. We see them as an investment into our quilting journey.

The Creative Grids Non-Slip Flying Geese & 45°/90° Triangle is an incredibily versatile 'all in one' ruler and my goodness - what a lot you can do with it! This ruler not only makes the flying geese unit a breeze to cut and put together but it also has so many more features that make it an extremely useful ruler indeed. You can of course use any other flying geese ruler so long as it has similar markings, but for the purpose of our book we use the Creative Grids Flying Geese & 45°/90° Triangle.

Apart from making flying geese units, you can use the 45° triangle on this ruler to make half-square triangle units. If you have read any of our jelly roll quilt books you will know how much we like that unit! We have shown you how to make half-square triangle units in our quilt *Bajan Sunset*. You can also make quarter-square triangles using the 90° section and you can also put the 90° section to work on different techniques to create quick and fun quilts. We have included the *Geometric Breeze* quilt in this book to show you how to use this ruler for some very clever 'strip tube' cutting.

Making quilts is fun and addictive. We really hope this book gives you a huge dose of inspiration and that you enjoy making the quilts. We are sure that once you get started with the flying geese unit you will become totally hooked like us!

Pam & Nicky

The Flying Geese Unit

The flying geese unit is made up of a 90° centre triangle with a 45° triangle on each side. It is important to understand the difference between a 90° triangle and a 45° triangle as they look pretty similar.

When cutting at any 45° angle you create a bias edge and bias edges tend to stretch if not handled with care. Many people use spray starch to stabilise bias edges when sewing and, although we don't tend to do this, it can be very helpful. One thing you should always remember is to press bias edges gently and never use steam. The important thing however is that you don't end up with outer bias edges. The aim is always to have straight edges on the outside edges of your blocks.

The 90° centre triangle of a flying geese unit has straight edges top and bottom and bias edges on the sides. The 45° side triangles, however, have straight edges on the two sides which form the outside of the unit. The bias edge of the 45° triangle is sewn to the bias edge of the centre triangle. Mission accomplished – we have a unit which has straight edges on all four sides when sewn.

Have a look at the diagrams here - this will help it all make sense!

To help you understand the angles of the triangles in the flying geese block, take some time to look at the diagrams below which show you the bias and straight edges.

90° triangle

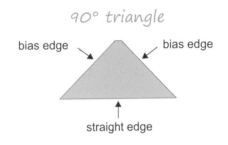

bias edge · bias edge · straight edge

45° triangle

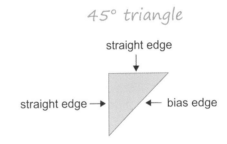

straight edge · straight edge · bias edge

Flying Geese Unit

all four sides have straight edges

All our patterns are based on fabric being 42in wide.
We cannot stress enough the importance of maintaining an accurate scant ¼in seam allowance throughout. Please take the time to test your seam allowance with the test in the General Instructions.
Please read through all the instructions before starting your quilt.

Flying Geese
the multi-size way

featuring Creative Grids Multi-Size Flying Geese & 45°/90° Triangle designed by Rachel Cross

The Multi-Size Flying Geese & 45°/90° Triangle (Creative Grids code CGRMSFG4590) enables you to make the traditional flying geese unit easily and accurately in sizes from 1in x 2in to 6in x 12in.

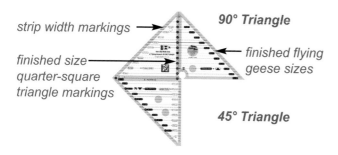

The 90° triangle also enables you to make quarter-square triangles and the 45° triangle enables you to make half-square triangles. This makes this ruler VERY USEFUL indeed!

When using the 90° triangle for the centres of the flying geese units, align the correct strip width line along the bottom of the strip and the cut off top of the triangle along the top. Cut the first triangle.

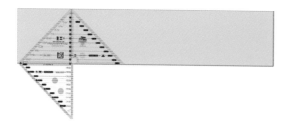

Rotate the ruler 180° and cut the next triangle. Continue along the strip to cut the required number of triangles.

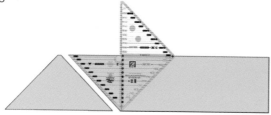

When using the 45° triangle for the side triangles of the flying geese units, **FOLD THE FABRIC STRIP IN HALF.** This enables you to cut the right and left triangles at the same time. Align the correct strip width line along the bottom of the strip and the cut off top of the triangle along the top. Cut the first pair of triangles.

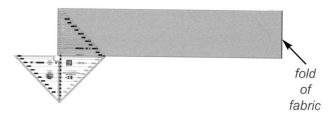

Rotate the ruler 180° and cut the next pair of triangles. Continue along the strip to cut the required number of triangles. Note the keyhole gap that allows this cutting.

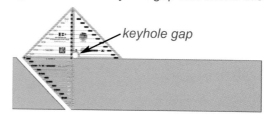

Notice that the 90° centre triangle has a cut off top and the 45° triangles have one cut off point.

When sewing the half-square triangles to the centre triangles make sure you always have the cut off points matching. They will match either on the right side of the centre triangle or on the left side.

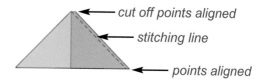

When sewing two flying geese units together you need your stitching line to be to the right of the point so you don't cut off the tip of the triangle.

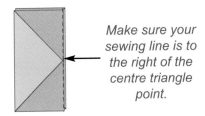

Make sure your sewing line is to the right of the centre triangle point.

correct

incorrect

We would like to say here just once that there are no 'point police' on duty. Our aim is to have perfect points and that is what we strive to achieve. If a point has gone wrong and really offends you then it is quite easy to undo a few stitches and re-sew the seam. However, please remember that we are not all perfect and quiltmaking is meant to be fun. If a few imperfect points slip through then it is not the end of the world – it really is true that no one else will notice them.

CUTTING TABLE

This table will help you calculate fabric requirements if you feel inspired to create your own quilt designs using either the Multi-Size Flying Geese & 45°/90° Triangle or a similar speciality flying geese ruler.

strip width x 42in	finished size of flying geese units	number of 90° centre triangles cut from one strip	number of pairs of 45° triangles cut from one strip. FOLD STRIPS so right and left triangles are cut together.
2in	1½in x 3in	14	14
2½in	2in x 4in	12	12
3in	2½in x 5in	11	11
3½in	3in x 6in	9	9
4in	3½in x 7in	8	8
4½in	4in x 8in	7	7
5in	4½in x 9in	6	6
5½in	5in x 10in	6	6
6in	5½in x 11in	5	5
6½in	6in x 12in	5	5

Flight to Paradise

In our Flight to Paradise quilt we have used virtually every measurement there is on our Creative Grids Multi-Size Flying Geese & 45°/90° triangle. We couldn't resist trying out all the sizes to see what they looked like and then decided they looked quite interesting altogether. That's sometimes the way quilts get designed! Don't be daunted by the long cutting instructions – we just wanted to make it very clear. You are doing exactly the same thing all the time but just with different size strips.

Vital Statistics:

Quilt Size:	60in x 74in
No. of Blocks:	ten each of nine different size flying geese blocks
Setting:	5 vertical rows + 2in centre sashing

Requirements:

- You need nine fabrics grading from dark (colour 1) to light (colour 9) or, if you wish to use just one fabric, you need a total of 2½ yards (2.25m)

Colour 1:	⅛ yard (10cms)
Colour 2:	⅛ yard (10cms)
Colour 3:	⅛ yard (10cms)
Colour 4:	¼ yard (20cms)
Colour 5:	⅜ yard (25cms)
Colour 6:	⅜ yard (30cms)
Colour 7:	⅜ yard (30cms)
Colour 8:	⅝ yard (50cms)
Colour 9:	⅝ yard (60cms)

- Background fabric 4 yards (3.75m)
- Binding fabric ½ yard (50cms)

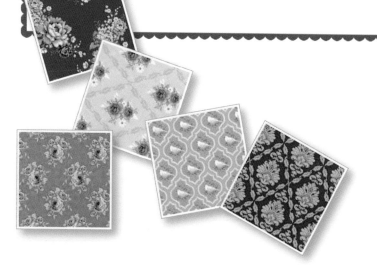

We used a selection of gorgeous aqua and blue fabric mostly from the wonderful Tilda collections by Tone Finnengar. However, there are a few other fabrics added to the quilt. Sometimes we get quite particular about using fabrics from the same collection - but don't be, it's good fun to mix them up!
Pieced by the authors and longarm quilted by The Quilt Room on a Gammill Statler Stitcher.

Cutting Instructions for colours 1-9

Colour 1 (darkest)
1 Cut one 2½in strip across the width of the fabric.
Using the 90° triangle and lining up the **2½in strip line**
(finished size 2in x 4in) with the bottom of the strip cut
ten 90° triangles, rotating the ruler 180° as you cut.

10 2in x 4in

Colour 2
2 Cut one 3in strip across the width of the fabric.
Using the 90° triangle and lining up the **3in strip line**
(finished size 2½in x 5in) with the bottom of the strip cut
ten 90° triangles, rotating the ruler 180° as you cut.

10 2½in x 5in

Colour 3
3 Cut one 3½in strip across the width of the fabric.
Using the 90° triangle and lining up the **3½in strip line**
(finished size 3in x 6in) with the bottom of the strip cut
ten 90° triangles, rotating the ruler 180° as you cut.

10 3in x 6in

Colour 4
4 Cut two 4in strips across the width of the fabric.
Using the 90° triangle and lining up the **4in strip line**
(finished size 3½in x 7in) with the bottom of the strips
cut ten 90° triangles, rotating the ruler 180° as you cut.

10 3½in x 7in

Colour 5
5 Cut two 4½in strips across the width of the fabric.
Using the 90° triangle and lining up the **4½in strip line**
(finished size 4in x 8in) with the bottom of the strips cut
ten 90° triangles, rotating the ruler 180° as you cut.

10 4in x 8in

Colour 6
6 Cut two 5in strips across the width of the fabric.
Using the 90° triangle and lining up the **5in strip line**
(finished 4½in x 9in) with the bottom of the strips cut
ten 90° triangles, rotating the ruler 180° as you cut.

10 4½in x 9in

Colour 7
7 Cut two 5½in strips across the width of the fabric.
Using the 90° triangle and lining up the **5½in strip line**
(finished size 5in x 10in) with the bottom of the strips
cut ten 90° triangles, rotating the ruler 180° as you cut.

10 5in x 10in

Colour 8
8 Cut three 6in strips across the width of the fabric.
Using the 90° triangle and lining up the **6in strip line**
(finished size 5½in x 11in) with the bottom of the strips
cut ten 90° triangles, rotating the ruler 180° as you cut.

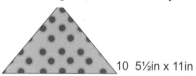

10 5½in x 11in

Colour 9 (lightest)
9 Cut three 6½in strips across the width of the fabric.
Using the 90° triangle and lining up the **6½in strip line**
(finished size 6in x 12in) with the bottom of the strips
cut ten 90° triangles, rotating the ruler 180° as you cut.

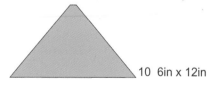

10 6in x 12in

Flight to Paradise

Cutting Instructions for background fabric

10 *Cut six 2½in strips across the width of the fabric.*
- Set two strips aside for the centre sashing strip.
- Using the 45° triangle, line up the **2½in strip line** with the bottom of one **folded** strip and cut **ten pairs** of 2in 45° triangles, rotating the ruler 180° as you cut.
- Cut twenty 2½in x 4½in rectangles from three strips.
- Put the triangles and rectangles together in a pile with the 90° triangles from colour 1 fabric.

10 pairs of 2in 45° triangles

11 *Cut three 3in strips across the width of the fabric.*
- Using the 45° triangle, line up the **3in strip line** with the bottom of one **folded** strip and cut **10 pairs** of 2½in 45° triangles, rotating the ruler 180° as you cut.
- Cut twenty 3in x 4in rectangles from two strips.
- Put the triangles and rectangles together in a pile with the 90° triangles from colour 2 fabric.

10 pairs of 2½in 45° triangles

12 *Cut three 3½in strips across the width of the fabric.*
- Using the 45° triangle, line up the **3½in strip line** with the bottom of one **folded** strip and cut **10 pairs** of 3in 45° triangles, rotating the ruler 180° as you cut.
- Cut twenty 3½in x 3½in squares from two strips.
- Put the triangles and squares together in a pile with the 90° triangles from colour 3 fabric.

10 pairs of 3in 45° triangles

13 *Cut four 4in strips across the width of the fabric.*
- Using the 45° triangle, line up the **4in strip line** with the bottom of two **folded** strips and cut **10 pairs** of 3½in 45° triangles, rotating the ruler 180° as you cut.
- Cut twenty 3in x 4in rectangles from two strips.
- Put the triangles and rectangles together in a pile with the 90° triangles from colour 4 fabric.

10 pairs of 3½in 45° triangles

14 *Cut four 4½in strips across the width of the fabric.*
- Using the 45° triangle, line up the **4½in strip line** with the bottom of two **folded** strips and cut **10 pairs** of 4in 45° triangles, rotating the ruler 180° as you cut.
- Cut twenty 2½in x 4½in rectangles from two strips.
- Put the triangles and rectangles together in a pile with the 90° triangles from colour 5 fabric.

10 pairs of 4in 45° triangles

15 *Cut three 5in strips across the width of the fabric.*
- Using the 45° triangle, line up the **5in strip line** with the bottom of two **folded** strips and cut **10 pairs** of 4½in 45° triangles, rotating the ruler 180° as you cut.
- Cut twenty 2in x 5in rectangles from two strips.
- Put the triangles and rectangles together in a pile with the 90° triangles from colour 6 fabric.

10 pairs of 4½in 45° triangles

16 *Cut three 5½in strips across the width of the fabric.*
- Using the 45° triangle, line up the **5½in strip line** with the bottom of two **folded** strips and cut **10 pairs** of 5in 45° triangles, rotating the ruler 180° as you cut.
- Cut twenty 1½in x 5½in rectangles from two strips.
- Put the triangles and rectangles together in a pile with the 90° triangles from colour 7 fabric.

10 pairs of 5in 45° triangles

17 *Cut three 6in strips across the width of the fabric.*
- Using the 45° triangle, line up the **6in strip line** with the bottom of two **folded** strips and cut **10 pairs** of 5½in 45° triangles, rotating the ruler 180° as you cut.
- Cut twenty 1in x 6in rectangles from two strips.
- Put the triangles and rectangles together in a pile with the 90° triangles from colour 8 fabric.

10 pairs of 5½in 45° triangles

18 *Cut two 6½in strips across the width of the fabric.*
- Using the 45° triangle, line up the **6½in strip line** with the bottom of two **folded** strips and cut **10 pairs** of 6in 45° triangles, rotating the ruler 180° as you cut.
- Put these in a pile with the 90° triangles from colour 9 fabric.

10 pairs of 6in 45° triangles

Cutting Instructions for binding

19 Cut seven 2½in wide strips across the width of the fabric.

1 Working with the pile of colour 1 triangles, take one colour 1 90° triangle and sew a 2in background 45° triangle cut from a 2½in strip to one side. Press as shown.

2 Sew another 2in background 45° triangle to the other side and press

3 Sew two 2½in x 4½in background rectangles to both sides of this unit and press. Repeat to make ten of these units.

4 Repeat steps 1-3 with the remaining size centre triangles to make ten units from each colourway, making sure you sew the correct size rectangles to each flying geese unit.

5 Sew one unit from each size flying geese together as shown to make one vertical row. Repeat to make ten vertical rows.

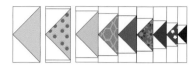

6 Sew five vertical rows together as shown, rotating the second and fourth rows 180° to make one half of the quilt. Repeat with the remaining five vertical rows to make an identical second half.

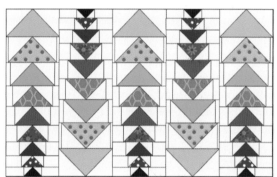

make 2

Assembling the Quilt

7 Measure the width of these units. Sew two 2½in sashing strips together and then trim to this measurement.

Rotate one unit 180° and sew the two units together with the 2½in sashing strip in between. Press.

8 Your quilt top is now complete. Quilt and bind as desired.

Flight to Paradise

Trade Winds

These large quilt blocks are quick to piece and are made from 5in x 10in flying geese units sewn around a centre square. We then made smaller 3in x 6in flying geese units to create the border. Our fabric requirements are given as the total yardage of the colours required but as always we love to use as many fabrics as possible. If you wish your quilt to be as scrappy as ours then cut your strips from a variety of fabrics within the same colourway.

Vital Statistics:
Quilt Size:	60in x 75in
Block Size:	15in
No. of blocks:	12
Setting:	3 x 4 blocks with 1½in inner border and 6in flying geese border.

Requirements:
- Red fabric: 1⅝ yards (1.50m)
- Green fabric: 1¼ yards (1.10m)
- Background: 2½ yards (2.40m)

Cutting Instructions

Don't forget to rotate your ruler 180° after each cut.

Red fabric:
1 Cut nine 3½in strips across the width of the fabric.
- Using the 45° triangle and lining up the **3½in strip line** with the bottom of the **folded** strips, cut nine pairs of 3in 45° triangles from each strip. You need 74 pairs in total so seven pairs are spare.

74 pairs of red 3in 45° triangles

2 Cut four 5½in strips across the width of the fabric.
- Using the 45° triangle and lining up the **5½in strip line** with the bottom of the **folded** strips, cut six pairs of 5in 45° triangles from each strip. You need 24 pairs in total.

24 pairs of red 5in 45° triangles

Green fabric:
3 Cut six 2in strips across the width of the fabric and set these aside for the inner border.

4 Cut one 6½in strip across the width of the fabric. Subcut into four 6½in squares for the border corners.

5 Cut four 5½in strips across the width of the fabric.
- Using the 45° triangle and lining up the **5½in strip line** with the bottom of the **folded** strips, cut six pairs of 5in 45° triangles from each strip. You need 24 pairs in total.

24 pairs of green 5in 45° triangles

Background fabric:
6 Cut ten 5½in strips across the width of the fabric.
- Take two 5½in strips and subcut each strip into six 5½in squares to make a total of twelve squares for the block centres.
- Using the 90° triangle and lining up the **5½in strip line** with the bottom of the strips, cut six 90° triangles from each of the remaining eight strips. You need a total of 48.

48 5in x 10in 90° triangles

7 Cut nine 3½in strips across the width of the fabric.
- Using the 90° triangle and lining up the **3½in strip line** with the bottom of the strip, cut nine 90° triangles from each strip. Repeat with all nine strips to make a total of eighty-one. You need 74 so seven are spare.

74 3in x 6in 90° triangles

1 Sew one 5in green 45° triangle to one side of the 5in x 10in background centre triangle as shown and press.

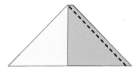

2 Repeat on the other side and press.

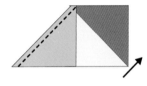

3 Repeat to make 24 **green** 5in x 10in flying geese units.

Make 24

4 Repeat to make twenty-four red 5in x 10in flying geese units.

Make 24

5 Repeat with the 3in **red** 45° triangles and 3in x 6in background 90° triangles to make 74 3in x 6in flying geese units for the borders.

Make 74

6 Take four red 5in x 10in flying geese units and one 5½in background square. With right sides together, partially sew one flying geese unit along the top of the square as shown, starting the seam approximately in the centre of the 5½in square. Carefully press open and this will create a straight edge to sew the next flying geese unit.

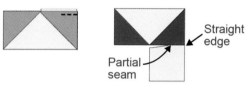

Straight edge

Partial seam

7 Sew another 5in x 10in flying geese unit down the right hand side as shown. Press open.

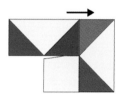

8 Sew another 5in x 10in flying geese unit along the bottom and press open.

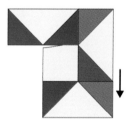

9 Sew the fourth 5in x 10in flying geese unit in place and press open. Then complete the partial seam to complete the block. Press.

Complete seam

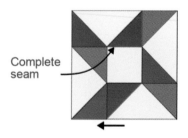

10 Repeat to make six red blocks and six green blocks.

Adding the Borders

11 Join the six 2in wide green strips and sew into a continuous length. Cut two lengths of 60½in which is the vertical measurement of your quilt and sew these to the sides of your quilt, easing if necessary. Press.

12 Cut two lengths of 48½in which is the horizontal measurement of your quilt and sew to the top and bottom, easing if necessary. Your quilt will now measure 48½in x 63½in and this is important to ensure your flying geese border fits nicely.

13 Sew twenty-one 3in x 6in flying geese units together. Repeat to make two of these rows for your side borders. Press seams in one direction.

14 Sew sixteen 3in x 6in flying geese units together as shown and sew a 6½in green square to both ends. Repeat to make two of these rows. Press seams in one direction.

15 Pin and sew the side borders on first, easing if necessary. Make sure the flying geese are pointing in the right direction. Press and then sew the top and bottom borders on last again making sure the flying geese are pointing in the right direction.

16 Your quilt is now complete. Quilt as desired and bind to finish.

Jet Stream Jewel

When we were asked to make a quilt to showcase some gorgeous hand-marbled fabric, we jumped at the chance. This is such a simple quilt, which is brought alive by the unique designs created by the hand-marbled fabric. If you want to showcase any fabric you love then this is a quick and easy quilt pattern to follow. A large-scale fabric would also be good to use as the different sections of the fabric will vary in each block.

Vital Statistics:

Quilt Size:	38in x 45in
Block Size:	3½in x 7in
No. of blocks:	40
Setting:	4 vertical rows of 10 blocks + 5in border

Requirements:

•	Fabric to showcase	⅝ yards (60cms)
•	Fabric for background	⅝ yards (60cms)
•	Fabric for borders	⅝ yards (60cms)

Our background and border fabric were the same.

Cutting Instructions

Fabric to showcase:
• Cut five 4in strips across the width of the fabric. Using the 90° triangle and lining up the **4in strip line** with the bottom of the strips, cut eight 90° triangles from each of the five strips for the centres of the flying geese units. Rotate your ruler 180° after each cut. You need a total of forty.

40
3½in x 7in
90° triangles

Fabric for background:
• Cut five 4in strips across the width of the fabric.
• Using the 45° triangle and lining up the **4in strip line** with the bottom of the *folded* strips, cut eights pairs of 3½in 45° triangles from each strip. Rotate your ruler 180° after each cut. You need forty pairs in total.

40 pairs
of 3½in 45°
background triangles

Fabric for border:
• Cut four 5½in strips across the width of the fabric.

Assembling the Flying Geese Units

1 Sew one background 45° triangle to one side of the flying geese centre triangle, as shown, and then press.

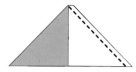

2 Repeat on the other side and then press away from the centre triangle.

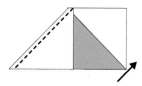

3 Repeat to make forty 3½in x 7in flying geese units.

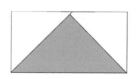

Make 40

18

4 Take two flying geese units and, with right sides together, sew together. Arrange your two units so that you are can see the tip of the triangle over which you are sewing. You do not want your stitching line to cut off the point of the triangle.

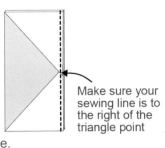

Make sure your sewing line is to the right of the triangle point

5 Sew ten flying geese units together to form one vertical row. Press two with seams pressed down and press two with seams pressed up. This will mean that the seams will nest together nicely when sewing the rows together.

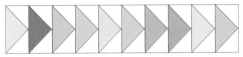

6 Sew the four vertical rows together, pinning at every seam intersection to ensure a perfect match.

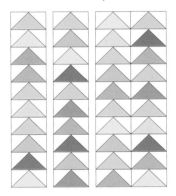

Adding the Borders

7 Determine the vertical measurement from top to bottom through the centre of your quilt top. Trim two side border strips to this measurement. Mark the halves and quarters of one quilt side and one border with pins. Placing right sides together and matching the pins, stitch quilt and border together, easing to fit where necessary. Repeat on the opposite side. Press open.

8 Determine the horizontal measurement from side to side across the centre of the quilt top. Trim two top and bottom border strips to this measurement and add to the quilt top in the same manner.

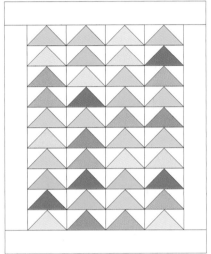

9 Your quilt is now complete. Quilt as desired and bind to

Bajan Sunset

Using a combination of three different blocks, all containing flying geese units, half-square triangle units and squares, you can create this complex looking quilt. Be organised and make all your units at the start and then lay them out in separate piles by your sewing machine.

Our quilt looks very scrappy but in fact we used only four different half metres. This is one of the benefits of using large-scale prints because when they are cut up into smaller pieces they all look so different. This quilt also shows how to use the flying geese ruler to make half-square triangle units.

Vital Statistics:
Quilt Size: 60in x 60in
Block Size: 18in
No. of blocks: 9
Setting: 3 x 3 blocks + 3in border

Requirements:
- Four ½ yards/metres of large scale red/orange fabrics
- 2⅝ yards (2.5m) purple fabric

Eddystone Light

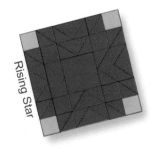

Rising Star

Cup and Saucer

We told you this was a veratile ruler. In this quilt we use it to make our flying geese units plus we also use it to make our half-square triangle units.

This quilt uses fabrics by Kaffe Fassett. We love his large prints which when cut into small pieces take on a whole new look. We decided on a purple co-ordinating fabric to really help enrich the quilt and make the blocks come alive. Pieced by the authors and longarm quilted by The Quilt Room on a Gammill Statler Stitcher.

Cutting Instructions

Red/orange fabric:

- Cut each half yard into five 3½in wide strips across the width of the fabric to make a total of twenty 3½in strips.

  – Take five 3½in strips and using the 90° triangle, line up the **3½in strip line** (finished size 3in x 6in) with the bottom of the strip and cut the first triangle. Rotating the ruler along the strip, cut eight 90° triangles from each strip. Repeat with all five strips to make a total of forty 3in x 6in 90° triangles.

  40
  3in x 6in
  90° triangles

  – Take six 3½in strips and using the 45° triangle line up the **3½in strip line** on the ruler with the bottom of the **folded** strips and cut eight pairs of 3in 45° triangles from each strip, rotating the ruler 180° after each cut. You need forty-eight pairs of 3in 45° triangles in total.

  48 pairs of
  3in 45° triangles

  – Take five 3½in strips and cut twelve 3½in squares from each strip to make a total of sixty.

  60
  3½in squares

  – Leave four 3½in strips uncut to make the red and purple half-square triangle units.

- **Purple fabric:**
  Cut one 6½in strip across the width of the fabric and subcut into five 6½in squares.

- Cut twenty-three 3½in strips across the width of the fabric.

  – Take six 3½in strips and using the 90° triangle, line up the **3½in strip line** (finished size 3in x 6in) with the bottom of the strip and cut the first triangle. Rotating the ruler along the strip, cut eight 90° triangles from each strip. Repeat with all six strips to make a total of forty-eight 3in x 6in 90° triangles.

  48
  3in x 6in
  90° triangles

  – Take five 3½in strips and using the 45° triangle line up the **3½in strip line** on the ruler with the bottom of the **folded** strips and cut eight pairs of triangles from each strip, rotating the ruler 180° after each cut. You need forty pairs of 3in 45° triangles in total.

  40 pairs of
  3in 45° triangles

  – Take eight 3½in strips and cut one 3½in x 24½in rectangle and two 3½in squares from each strip to make a total of eight 3½in x 24½in rectangles and sixteen 3½in squares. The balance of these strips is spare.

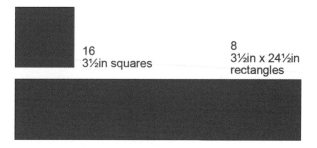

  16
  3½in squares

  8
  3½in x 24½in
  rectangles

- Leave four 3½in strips uncut to make the red and purple half-square triangle units.

Sewing Instructions

Making the Flying Geese Units

1 Sew one purple 45° triangle to one side of a red 90° triangle, and then press open as shown.

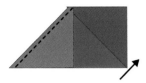

2 Repeat on the other side and press open to form flying geese Unit A. Repeat to make forty Unit A.

Make 40
flying geese –
Unit A

3 Sew one red 3in 45° triangle to one side of a purple 90° triangle and press open as shown.

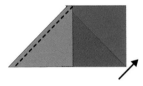

4 Repeat on the other side and press open to form flying geese Unit B. Repeat to make forty-eight Unit B.

Make 48
flying geese –
Unit B

Making the Half-Square Triangle Units

5 Take a 3½in red strip and a 3½in purple strip and press right sides together ensuring that they are exactly one on top of the other. The pressing will help hold the two strips together.

6 Lay them out on a cutting mat and position the 45° triangle as shown, lining up the **3½in strip line** with the bottom edge of the strips. Trim the selvedge and cut the first triangle. Rotate the ruler 180° and cut the next triangle. Continue along the strip to cut sixteen pairs of triangles from each strip.

3½in strip line

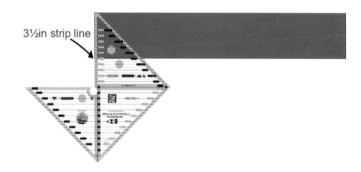

7 Sew along the diagonal of each pair of triangles. Trim the dog ears and press open towards the dark fabric to form sixteen half-square triangle units. Repeat with all four red strips and four purple strips allocated for the half-square triangle units. You need sixty-four half-square triangle units in total.

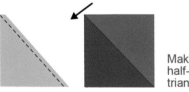

Make 64
half-square
triangle units

8 You need to make four **Rising Star** blocks.
Choose the following for each of the four blocks:
- Eight flying geese Unit A
- Eight half-square triangle units
- Eight red/orange 3½in squares
- One purple 6½in square

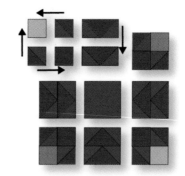

Piecing the block:
9 Sew the flying geese Unit As together and press as shown.

10 Sew the corner units together and press as shown, pinning at every seam intersection to ensure a perfect match.

11 Sew the units into rows and sew the rows together, pressing rows in alternate directions wherever possible so the seams nest together nicely.

12 Repeat to make four Rising Star blocks..

Making the Cup & Saucer Blocks

13 You need to make four **Cup and Saucer** blocks.
Choose the following for each of the four blocks.
- Ten flying geese Unit B
- Eight half-square triangle units
- Four red/orange 3½in squares
- Four purple 3½in squares

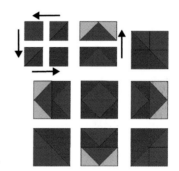

Piecing the block:
14 Sew the flying geese Unit Bs together and press as shown.

15 Sew the corner units together pinning at every seam intersection to ensure a perfect match. Press as shown.

16 Sew the units into rows and then sew the rows together, pressing rows in alternate directions wherever possible so the seams nest together nicely.

17 Repeat the process to make four Cup and Saucer blocks.

Making the Eddystone Light Block

18 You need to make one **Eddystone Light** block.
Choose the following for the block.
- Four flying geese Unit A
- Eight flying geese Unit B
- Eight red/orange 3½in squares
- One purple 6½in square

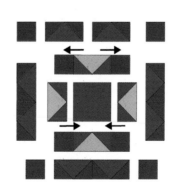

Piecing the block:
19 Sew a flying geese Unit A to both sides of the 6½in purple square as shown and press to the centre.

20 Sew a 3½in red square to both sides of two flying geese Unit As, pressing to the squares. Sew this unit to the top and bottom of the centre unit.

21 Sew the outer flying geese Unit Bs as shown and sew to both sides of the centre unit.

22 Join the top and bottom rows and sew to the top and bottom of the centre unit, pinning at every seam intersection to ensure a perfect match.

Assembling the Quilt

1 Lay out the nine blocks with the Eddystone Light block in the centre and the Rising Star blocks in the four corners. When you are happy with the arrangement, sew the blocks into rows, pinning at every seam intersection to ensure a perfect match. Press rows 1 and 3 to the left and row 2 to the right, so the seams will nest together nicely when sewing the rows together.

2 Now sew the rows together, pinning at every seam intersection. Press the seams.

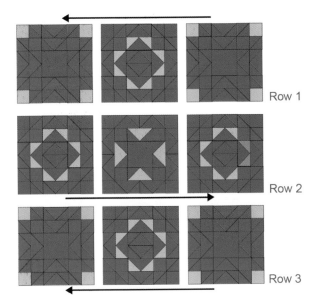

Row 1

Row 2

Row 3

3 Pin and sew the side borders on first, easing where necessary, and then press. Sew the top and bottom borders on, easing where necessary and then press.

4 Your quilt top is now complete. Quilt as desired and bind to finish.

Adding the Borders

1 Sew two 3½in x 24½in rectangles to both sides of one flying geese Unit A. Repeat to make two side inner borders.

2 Sew two 3½in x 24½in rectangles to both sides of one flying geese Unit A and sew a red 3½in square to both ends. Repeat to make two for the top and bottom borders.

Side border – make 2

Top and bottom border – make 2

Coastal Paths

We have given yardage requirements for this quilt but if you have some spare jelly roll strips this is the perfect quilt to use them up as we used just sixteen 2½in wide strips and background fabric. We love the scrappy effect the jelly roll strips create in this quilt so if you do have some spare strips this is how to sort them. We used three different strips each of pink, blue, green and yellow, two different strips of grey plus one strip each of blue and green for sashing squares. Just add four yards of background fabric, mix well and hey presto – you have one beautiful quilt.

Vital Statistics:
Quilt Size: 61¼in x 61¼in
Block Size: 17¾in
No. of blocks: 9
Setting: 3 x 3 blocks + 2in border

Requirements:
- Long quarters of blue, green, yellow & pink
- Long quarter grey fabric
- Long quarter for sashing squares
- Background fabric - 4 yards (3.6m)
- Binding fabric - ⅝ yard (60cms)

Cutting Instructions

Blue, green, yellow and pink fabric:
- Cut each fabric into three 2½in wide strips across the width of the fabric to make a total of twelve strips.
- Take each of the strips and using the 90° triangle, line up the **2½in strip line** (finished size 2in x 4in) with the bottom of the strip. Cut twelve 90° triangles from each strip to make a total of 144 2in x 4in 90° triangles for the flying geese centres, rotating your ruler 180° as you cut. You will have thirty-six in each of the four colours.

144
2in x 4in
90º triangles

Grey fabric:
- Cut two 2½in wide strips across the width of the fabric. Using the 90° triangle, line up the **2½in strip line** (finished size 2in x 4in) with the bottom of the strips and cut a total of eighteen 2in x 4in 90° triangles for the flying geese centre triangles, rotating your ruler 180° as you cut.

18 grey
2in x 4in
90º triangles

Sashing squares:
- Cut two 2½in wide strips across the width of the fabric and subcut into a total of sixteen 2½in squares.

Background fabric:
- Cut twenty-six 2½in strips across the width of the fabric.

  - Take twelve 2½in strips and cut each strip into two 2½in x 18¼in rectangles to make a total of twenty-four sashing strips.

  - Take fourteen 2½in strips and using the 45° triangle, line up the **2½in strip line** with the bottom of the **folded** strips and cut twelve pairs of 2in 45° triangles from each strip, rotating your ruler 180° as you cut. You need 162 pairs in total so six pairs are spare.

162 pairs of
2in background
45º triangles

- Cut nine 6½in strips across the width of the fabric and using the 90° triangle line up the **6½in strip line** with the bottom of the strip and cut each strip into four 90° triangles to make a total of thirty-six setting triangles, rotating your ruler 180° as you cut.

36
6in setting
triangles

- Cut three 4in strips across the width of the fabrics. Using the 45° triangle, line up the **4in strip line** with the bottom of the strips and cut a total of thirty-six 45° triangles for the corners of the blocks, rotating your ruler 180° as you cut.

36
corner
triangles

Border fabric:
Cut six 2½in strips across the width of the fabric.

Binding fabric:
Cut seven 2½in strips across the width of the fabric

Sewing Instructions

Assembling the Flying Geese Units

1 Sew one background 45° triangle to one side of a 90° flying geese centre triangle, as shown and press.

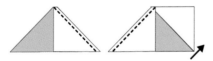

2 Repeat on the other side and press the flying geese unit.

3 Repeat to make thirty-six each of blue, green, pink and yellow flying geese units and eighteen grey flying geese units. Chain piecing will speed up this process (see General Instructions p 35).

Make 36
of each

Make 18

Assembling the Blocks

4 Take two grey flying geese units and, pinning at the seam intersections, sew together as shown to make a centre square. Repeat to make nine centre squares.

Make 9
centre squares

5 Take one each of the blue, green, pink and yellow units and sew them together as shown to make Unit A. Press. Repeat to make thirty-six Unit A.

Make 36
of Unit A

6 Sew two Unit As together, with a centre square in the middle to make the centre row of the block. Repeat to make nine centre rows.

Make 9
centre rows

7 Sew a setting triangle to both sides of a Unit A and press as shown. Repeat to make eighteen of these units. The setting triangles are cut slightly larger so when sewing the setting triangles make sure the bottom of the triangle is aligned with the bottom of the block.

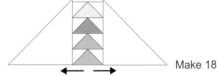

Make 18

8 Take two of these units and sew them together with a centre row in between. Pin at every seam intersection to ensure a perfect match. Repeat to make nine blocks.

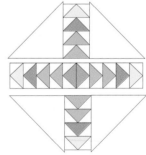

9 Sew on the corner triangles and trim to square up the blocks. The blocks should each measure 18¼in square.

Assembling the Quilt

10 Sew four 2½in x 18¼in sashing strips together with three blocks to make one row, as shown, and press as shown. Repeat to make three rows in total.

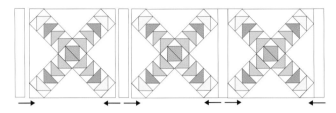

11 Sew three 2½in x 18¼in sashing strips together with four 2½in sashing squares. Press towards the sashing squares. Repeat to make four sashing strip rows.

12 Sew the three rows together with the four sashing strip rows as shown, pinning at every seam intersection to ensure a perfect match. Press the work.

13 Your quilt top is now complete. Quilt as desired and bind to finish.

You can really see the longarm quilting. We used a lovely dancing hearts pattern coupled with a neutral thread to let the pattern 'sink' into the quilts. We used a range of pastel colours but you could use a selection from just one colourway combined with background fabric. Pieced by the authors and longarm quilted by The Quilt Room on a Gammill Statler Stitcher.

# Geometric Breeze

Making flying geese units is such fun and using a ruler created specially for making them makes life so much easier. Speciality rulers, however, are sometimes even more clever than we think. Certainly the Creative Grids Multi-Size Flying Geese & 45°/90° Triangle can do lots more and we just wanted to give you a taster of what else it can do.

'Strip Tube Cutting' is a fun technique that creates a variety of effects and in this quilt we describe the technique and show you how to make two different blocks, which can be created to make a stunning quilt.

Vital Statistics:
Quilt Size: 55in x 55in
Block Size: 8½in
No. of blocks: 36
Setting: 6 x 6 blocks + 2in wide border

Requirements:
- 1 yard (90cms) blue fabric
- 1 yard (90cms) red fabric
- 1 yard (90cms) green fabric

(OR a jelly roll could be used to make a scrappier quilt but it would need to be divided into three colourways to provide twelve strips in each colourway)
- 1⅛ yards (1.10 metres) background and border fabric
- ½ yard (50cms) binding

Cutting Instructions

Blue, red and green fabric:
- Cut each fabric into twelve 2½in wide strips across the width of the fabric.

Background and border fabric:
- Cut four 6½in wide strips across the width of the fabric.

- Cut five 2½in wide strips across the width of the fabric and set aside for the borders.

Binding fabric:
- Cut six 2½in wide strips across the width of the fabric.

We love the bright and striking contrast our fabrics give us and this contrast really helps show off the geometric design. This is such a quick technique and one we have used time and time again as it produces such striking results! Pieced by the authors and longarm quilted by The Quilt Room on a Gammill Statler Stitcher.

Cutting Instructions

1 Take one strip from each colourway and sew together down the long sides as shown. Press the seams in one direction. Repeat to make twelve of these strip units **always keeping the colours in the same order.**

Make 12

2 Take two of the strip units and place them right sides together, rotating one strip unit 180°. Make sure the seams nest up against each other all the way along the strip unit – pin in place to stop any movement. Sew a scant ¼in seam along both sides of the strip unit to form a tube. Repeat to make four tubes.

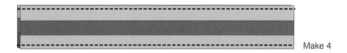
Make 4

3 Lay the 90° triangle on the tube as shown, lining up the **6½in strip line** along the bottom of the strip units. Cut either side of triangle.

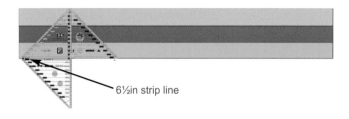
6½in strip line

4 Rotate the triangle along the tube to cut five triangles.

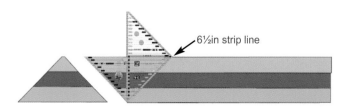
6½in strip line

5 Gently pick up each triangle and unpick the few threads that are along the tip of the triangle. You are dealing with **bias edges** now so care must be taken not to pull the fabric too much.

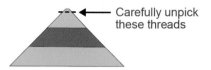
Carefully unpick these threads

6 Gently press open, pressing seams towards the blue fabric to make a total of twenty of these blocks.

Make 20

7 Using the remaining four strip units and the four 6½in wide background strips, place right sides together and sew a scant ¼in seam along both sides of the strip unit to form a tube. Repeat to make four tubes.

Make 4
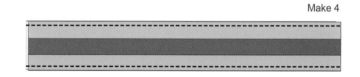

8 Using the 90° degree triangle as shown in steps 3 and 4, cut four triangles from each strip unit to make a total of sixteen triangles. Gently press open and press seams towards the background fabric. You will have eight each of two types of blocks, as shown.

Make 8

Make 8

Geometric Breeze

Assembling the Blocks

9 Referring to the diagram, arrange the blocks as shown, double checking that you have positioned them correctly. When you are happy with the arrangement sew the blocks into rows and then sew the rows together. Press the seams of alternate rows in opposite directions so that the seams nest together nicely when sewing the rows together.

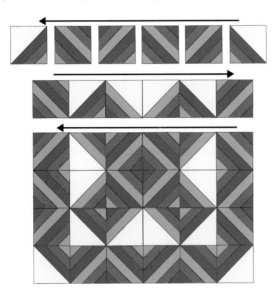

Adding the Borders

10 Join the border strips into a continuous length. Determine the vertical measurement from top to bottom through the centre of your quilt top. Cut two side borders to this measurement.

11 Mark the halves and quarters of one quilt side and one border with pins. Placing right sides together and matching the pins, stitch the quilt and border together, easing the quilt side to fit where necessary. Repeat on the opposite side. Press the seams.

12 Now determine the horizontal measurement from side to side across the centre of the quilt top. Cut two borders to this measurement. Pin and sew to the top and bottom of your quilt and press.

13 Your quilt is now complete. Quilt as desired and bind to finish.

 # General Instructions

Seam Allowance

We cannot stress enough the importance of maintaining an accurate ¼in seam allowance throughout. We prefer to say an accurate SCANT ¼in seam because there are two factors to take into consideration. Firstly, the thickness of thread and secondly when you press your seam allowance to one side, it takes up a tiny amount of fabric which has to be taken into consideration. These are both extremely small amounts but if they are ignored you will find your exact ¼in seam allowance is taking up more than ¼in.

It is well worth testing your seam allowance before starting on a quilt and most sewing machines have various needle positions which can be used to make any adjustments.

Seam Allowance Test

Cut three rectangles 2½in x 1½in. Sew two rectangles together down the longer side and press seam to one side. Sew the third rectangle across the top. It should fit exactly. If it doesn't, you need to make an adjustment to your seam allowance. If it is too long, your seam allowance is too wide and can be corrected by moving the needle on your sewing machine to the right. If it is too small, your seam allowance is too narrow and this can be corrected by moving the needle to the left.

This should fit exactly.

Pressing

In quiltmaking, pressing is of vital importance and if extra care is taken you will be well rewarded. We have a few tips to help you with your pressing.

- Always set your seam after sewing by pressing the seam as sewn, without opening up your unit/strips. This eases any tension and prevents the seam line from distorting.
- Move the iron with an up and down motion, zigzagging along the seam rather than ironing down the length of the seam which could cause distortion.
- Open up your unit/strips and press on the right side of the fabric towards the darker fabric, if necessary guiding the seam underneath to make sure the seam is going in the right direction.
- Always take care if using steam and certainly don't use steam anywhere near a bias edge.
- Unless there is a special reason for not doing so, seams are pressed towards the darker fabric. The main criteria when joining seams, however, is to have the seam allowances going in the opposite direction to each other as they then nest together without bulk. Your patchwork will lie flat and your seam intersections will be accurate.

Pinning

Don't underestimate the benefits of pinning. When you have to align a seam it is important to insert pins to stop any movement when sewing. Long, fine pins with flat heads are recommended as they will go through the layers of fabric easily and allow you to sew up to and over them. When aligning seams, insert a pin either at right angles or diagonally through the seam intersection ensuring that the seams are matching perfectly. When sewing, do not remove the pin too early as your fabric might shift and your seams will not be perfectly aligned.